The Truth About the Credit Reporting World

The Truth About the Credit Reporting World

Mark Guerrero

Copyright © 2011 by Mark Guerrero.

ISBN: Softcover   978-1-4628-6896-4

All rights reserved. No part of this book may be reproduced or transmitted in any form or by any means, electronic or mechanical, including photocopying, recording, or by any information storage and retrieval system, without permission in writing from the copyright owner.

This book was created in the United States of America.

To order additional copies of this book, contact:
Xlibris Corporation
1-888-795-4274
www.Xlibris.com
Orders@Xlibris.com
99002

CONTENTS

- ✓ How it all began? 8
- ✓ How Experian, Equifax, and TransUnion started? 9
- ✓ Just how sneaky the agencies were from the beginning? 10
- ✓ What the government did for you? 11
- ✓ What President Obama did for credit . . . ? 12
- ✓ What is not covered in the Credit CARD Act . . . ? 15
- ✓ What exactly is a FICO? 16
- ✓ The difference between a FICO and Vantage Score? 17
- ✓ There are secret credit scores!? 19
- ✓ Which bureaus use which score? 21
- ✓ Tthe credit bureaus sell your information? 22
- ✓ The more amounts of people have your information, the more your score goes down? 24
- ✓ You have the right to sue the credit bureaus? 25
- ✓ The credit bureaus aren't even in the U.S.!? 26
- ✓ The credit bureaus cannot always validate public record items? 27
- ✓ The burden of proof is on the consumer, not the creditor or collection agency? 28
- ✓ Credit bureaus want you to dispute online . . . . a huge NO,NO!? 30
- ✓ Credit bureaus put you into different scoring categories? 32
- ✓ How your score is broken down? 33
- ✓ The worse the score—the more money the credit bureaus make!!? 34
- ✓ Why the credit bureaus want inaccurate information? 35

- ✓ Canceling credit cards can actually hurt your credit score? 36
- ✓ What you can do to contest a credit item? 37
- ✓ The credit bureaus use a machine to read your letters?! 38
- ✓ There's a fourth secret credit bureau? 40
- ✓ Approximately 35% of your credit score is based on past debts that are over 30 days late? 42
- ✓ Never lie? 43
- ✓ Paying with cash and avoiding credit cards harms you even worse than having bad credit cards? 44
- ✓ Giving your teenager a credit card is a good choice? 45
- ✓ FREECREDITREPORT.COM IS NOT FREE!!!? 46
- ✓ What FDCPA violation is? 47
- ✓ Who or what are junk buyers? 49
- ✓ What is the statue of limitations on debt? 50
- ✓ Giving your teenager a credit card is a good choice? 51

Introduction

Let's face it we all need credit and at some point in our lives no matter how good our credit is unexpected things in 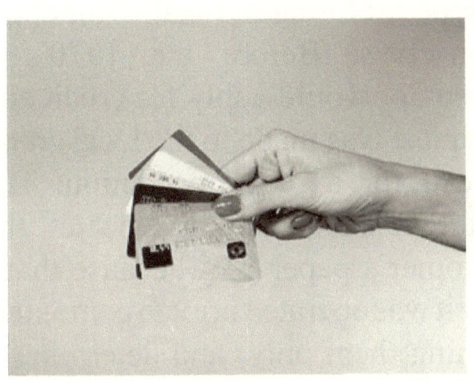 life come up and the truth is when it comes to priorities such as feeding your kids and paying your credit cards we can see which one wins. In today's economy especially with a growing unemployment rate no one's credit is unaffected. As credit is necessary to navigate the current economy, these flaws keep average citizens from purchasing a car, getting a job, and establishing utility services. Out of all the secrets that will be exposed in this book the one thing that is not a secret is that the current credit reporting system has flaws.

Despite the fact that these flaws are well documented and in most instances disputed, they continue to exist. It might even be said that the flaws actually make the current system fundamentally unsound, as they are so detrimental to the consumers and finance companies they claim to serve. Everything in this world is about making money and the credit system is set up for the credit card companies and the credit reporting companies to make the most money possible!

Did you know: how it all began?

In the beginning the credit agencies operated locally and got information on the consumer in all types of forms and share it amongst themselves. Before the 1970's a consumer would apply for credit and a request was made to the local credit bureau for a recommendation. The credit bureau would locate the customer's paper file (because that's how it was operated prior to computers running them only) and determine if he or she was a good credit risk and should be extended credit. At the time there wasn't a rating system or set criteria in place which provided a guideline for making such a recommendation. Unlike today, the consumer had no rights to view their credit file. If somehow the consumer caught wind of an error that existed in their credit file, there were no consumer protections in place to dispute erroneous information. If there was a questionable accounting in the file, a simple phone call or visit to the office could clear the matter up or explain it away.

During that time, credit bureaus would collect every bit of information they could about a person, including employment history, marital status, age, race, religion, testimonials, and any other information they could get their hands on. Information was also acquired from newspaper clippings, police blotter notations, tax filings, and statistics records. With all that information at their fingertips, discrimination occurred frequently, especially if the consumer was part of a certain ethnic group or resided in a certain neighborhood. This is how it all began!

Did you know: how Experian, Equifax, and TransUnion started?

Experian, was originally a defense contractor formally known as TRW, They began realizing the future importance of credit and pitched to local credit agencies the importance of conversion to electronic files and computers. They sparked the electronic age of credit files! Seeing as they were already a defense contractor they had the storage capabilities and could house all of the credit file information.

Equifax began as an insurance reporting business and realized that the business model could be applied to credit. As their business grew they turned to TRW to lease computer storage. TRW decided to raise their charges on the lease (not surprising) and Equifax eventually had to engineer their own system and servers.

TransUnion began as a medical record reporting company and also realized the future of credit. They struggled for several years and had a system that earned them a horrible reputation of misinformation and of being untrustworthy. The Federal Trade Commission, FTC, gave them the ultimatum to get rid of the existing system or to get out of the business of credit reporting. Trans Union bit the bullet and complied. In order to help establish themselves and fix their tarnished reputation they gave away credit reports for 3 years.

Did you know: just how sneaky the agencies were from the beginning?

We all have seen the nice gesture of neighbors welcoming someone a newcomer to the neighborhood by bringing over baked goods as a welcome gift and sitting down for impromptu introductions. Years ago, a well-known organization called the Welcome Wagon would do exactly this. Two to three women would prepare some baked goods and personally pay the new neighbor a visit at their home. Seems innocent enough right? They would sit and talk about  local activities and businesses, where the best deals at stores where, the best gas station prices, church, grocery stores and ask you about where you used to live. They would also look around the house, looking at furniture, decorations, children, and everything else you could imagine. The women would collect information on the unsuspecting homeowner. These women were not gossiping this information to the rest of the neighborhood. The Group "The Welcome Wagon" actually partnered with the credit bureaus to obtain and share the data, these women were actually employees of the local credit bureaus. Since they would also learn where you came from it was easy to order your file and then to add what they had learned. At the time, it was the only way the local bureaus could gather information.

Did you know: what the government did for you?

The Federal Government was receiving complaints about discrimination for home loans. They enacted the Fair Credit Reporting Act (FCRA) in 1971. The FCRA forced the credit reporting agencies to change the existing system of collecting 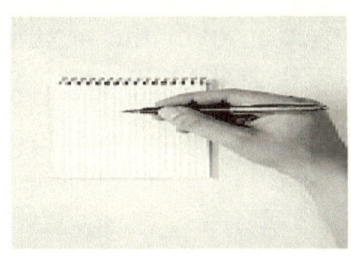 information and assessing credit worthiness. It regulates the collection, dissemination, and use of consumer information, including consumer credit information. Over time, the information in consumer reports became more reliable, but they were still so far from being an accurate reflection on the consumer's ability to manage credit.

Did you know: what President Obama did for credit . . . ?

President Obama signed the Credit Card Accountability, Responsibility and Disclosure Act (or Credit CARD Act) of 2009 recently. It includes the most sweeping changes in how credit cards are marketed, advertised and managed in decades.

Consumer protections will be phased in over the next 15 months with the earliest starting Aug. 20, 2009.

The law limits:

- when credit card interest rates can be increased on existing balances
- allows consumers whose interest rates have been increased to reduce their *annual percentage rates* (APRs) to previous levels if they've been good and paid their bills on time for six months
- Starting Aug. 20 2009, all card issuers must begin giving 45-day advance notice of significant changes in card terms.
- That is also the deadline for giving consumers at least 21 days (instead of the current 14) to pay their monthly credit card bills.

- The bulk of the consumer protections—limiting when interest rates can be increased, banning universal default and double-cycle billing, and restricting credit cards for minors, among others—take effect Feb. 22, 2010.
- Fines of up to $5,000 for card issuers that violate the act.
- Banning *universal default* and *double-cycle billing*.
- Prohibiting *over-limit fees* unless consumers agree to allow transactions that exceed their credit limits to go through rather than be denied.
- Fees for late payments, over-limit charges or other penalty fees must be reasonable and related to the violation.
- Extending the life of *gift cards and gift certificates* so that they cannot expire within five years of activation. Banning dormancy or inactivity fees on gift cards unless there has been no activity in a 12-month period.
- Banning credit cards for people under the age of 21 unless they have adult *co-signers* or show proof that they have the means to repay the debts.
  - College students must get permission from parents or guardians to increase credit limits on *joint accounts* they hold with those adults.
  - The new law will *ban those free pizza and T-shirt giveaways*—popular on many college campuses—if students sign up for credit cards. Colleges, universities and alumni associations would have to disclose the nature of contracts they sign with credit card marketers allowing access to student and alumni contact information.

- Requires that card issuers disclose how long it would take to pay off credit card balances if cardholders make only minimum payments each month and how much users would have to pay each month if they want to pay off their balances in 36 months.

Did you know: what is not covered in the Credit CARD Act . . . ?

Obama said the law is for "people who found out that credit cards are a one-way street. It's easy to get in but almost impossible to get out." He warned, however, that the law doesn't give consumers an easy pass: "We expect consumers to live within their means and pay what they owe," the president said.

Not covered:

- does not cap how high interest rates can go.
- does not limit when APRs can be hiked on future purchases.
- People with business or corporate credit cards will not have the same protections as people with personal credit cards because the new law and the federal rules apply only to consumer credit cards.
- The banking industry has said the new law would mean higher interest rates for all customers—including those who pay their bills on time and have good credit—and lowered credit limits or no credit cards at all for high risk customers with bad credit.
- *Annual fees* would also return as a routine component of many cards, according to issuers.

Did you know: what exactly is a FICO?

Lenders were under scrutiny from congress to establish a new system that would eliminate the complaints of discrimination and the credit bureaus had lost their credibility  and needed to do something to stay in business. Fair Isaac and company (now known as FICO) developed a solution. Released in the 1980s, they developed what was the first version of the rating system we know today as the FICO score. The system was welcomed but not for the benefits it offered the industry. Something had to be done to keep business moving forward, without further government regulation. Shocking! A decision that was made where the credit industry makes decisions based on what is best for the industry, not the consumer.

Lenders could now use the score to determine loan approvals faster and easier, this was great news for lenders but horrible news for consumers who were now being judged as numbers not as individuals.

Did you know: the difference between a FICO and Vantage Score?

The Vantage Score is the credit scoring risk model that was developed by Experian, Equifax and Transunion in order to compete with the FICO score. Why wouldn't they try and develop a new system to compete with a system that held them back from being even more corrupt?

FICO and VantageScore use two different ranges. The classic FICO scale runs from 300 to 850, while the VantageScore starts at 501 and runs to 990.

VantageScore breaks down like an elementary-school report card:

- **901-990** equals "A" credit
- **801-900** equals "B" credit
- **701-800** equals "C" credit
- **601-700** equals "D" credit
- **501-600** equals "F" credit

Although VantageScores are not practiced widely it is in the phase of consideration of whether it is better than the FICO. A little confused on which one you are being judged by? Don't worry; the lender will disclose the scoring system they are using if you ask . . . . . it's the least they could do.

Did you know: there are secret credit scores!?

The response score: this score basically predicts the likelihood a consumer will respond to an offer of credit, such as a new credit card or a balance transfer offer. Credit card ISSUERS use response score to decide whom to target and how to customize offers to appeal to particular consumers.

Application score: this score gathers information from your credit application that's not included in your credit scores, including how much you earn, how long you have live at your current address, and how long you have worked at your current employer. Application scores are often combined with other scores such as credit and bankruptcy scores to determine whether to open the account, what rate to give and how much credit to extend

Bankruptcy score: credit scores typically predict the chance you will miss a payment in the next two years. Bankruptcy scores predict the likelihood you will file for chapter 7 or chapter 3 payment plans. Equifax produces the leading bankruptcy navigator index (BNI). BNI's range from 1-300, with the higher score, the lower the predictor risk.

Revenue score: lenders want to maximize the profitability of each account and one way they do that is to gauge how much money each account is likely to generate.

Attrition risk score: attrition risk refers to the likelihood a user will stop using a credit card, attrition risk scores are typically used in combination with other scores to determine what to do next if they look ready to bolt.

Behavior score: behavior score typically focuses on a single account but take in a broad view. Does a user pay off bills each month, carry a balance, etc . . . or pay only the minimum on card? That information often is not available in a credit report. But is contained in the issuers databases along with other data that helps the score describe how single accounts are handled.

Collection score: these agencies use collection score to assess the likelihood that you will be able to pay them and sort their list of debtors accordingly. Collection agencies watch for all evidence that your financial situation may be improving.

Did you know: which bureaus use which score?

Experian only makes vantage scores available to the public, while TransUnion, and Equifax use FICO. But don't let this fool you, these bureaus ARE trying to get the Vantage Score system into effect. Experian is the one that took the leap for all three in 2009 by stopping all sales of FICO scores to consumers. Many assume this move is to bring Vantage Score a more widely known name by showing it being put to use.

What does this mean for you exactly? Watch your back is what it means!!! Plans for both risk-scoring models when working on your credit score. Seeing as this model really wasn't developed with the consumer in mind and utilizing it will benefit the banks and credit reporting bureaus the VantageScore gives lenders the capability to charge consumers more interest, so they will surely employ it when it serves their wellbeing.

Did you know: the credit bureaus sell your information?

There is a fee that the creditors pay to the credit bureaus when reporting negative credit items. The more negative items, the more money! It benefits them for those negative items to stay on your credit report because they are getting paid for those items.

The credit bureaus sell your information to those who are looking to give you credit. Obviously there are no more welcome wagons knocking on your door but there are so many other ways of obtaining data on consumers now. Data pirates include: collection agencies, credit card companies, banks, student loan providers, utility companies and finance companies. Not only do credit bureaus purchase information from these furnishers, they purchase the information from one another!

Consumers give up information to these companies without even realizing it. Think about it, you go and apply for a credit card, fill out all the information on the application. Now they now have what they need! Now comes step two, we obtain credit, we continue to give them information based on our payment habits. When a lender summits a request for a consumer credit report, the reporting agency forwards the information electronically. The process has been systemized so no human actually has to have any interaction.

Did you know: the more amounts of people have your information, the more your score goes down?

According to the FCRA—anyone that obtains a copy of your credit report must be noted on your report. If there is a frequent amount of inquiries on your credit report the FICO scoring model considers frequent inquiries as an indication that the consumer is actively seeking credit and possibly a greater risk. FICO also determines consumers as risks and are not demonstrating good judgment if they apply for too many lines of credit

There is a way of opting out so that no one is able to sell your information. This makes your file less valuable to them and by doing so it makes it easier to repair your credit.

OPT OUT NUMBER:

1-888-567-8688

Stops and prevent credit inquiries and solicitation without your permission for at least a minimal period of one year.

Did you know: you have the right to sue the credit bureaus?

Just like anything else in life if the law is broken you have the right to take them to court, they ARE NOT EXEMPT FROM LAW SUITS!!

Did you know: the credit bureaus aren't even in the U.S.!?

The credit bureaus are stationed outside of the United States, they have post offices boxes throughout the country with different addresses but they are not even here Experian, Equifax, and TransUnion are actually based out of the Philippines. Most people think that they are in the United States but they only have P.O. boxes throughout the United States. That's why they have so many different addresses.

Did you know: the credit bureaus cannot always validate public record items?

Especially in public record items, credit bureaus state that they have verified with the courts on public record items, but the fact is that most courts do not even do this! Some courts do not verify the information; they just are not setup to do it. The credit bureaus HAVE TO ABIDE by federal laws:

FCRA: The Fair Credit Reporting Act (FCRA) allows a consumer to challenge the information on his credit report on the basis of "completeness and accuracy." When a consumer files a dispute, the credit bureaus must contact the source of the credit information (the creditor) and confirm that the information is accurate, verifiable, and not obsolete. In some circumstances, the credit bureau is required to go beyond a simple verification of the creditor's own computer record. If, within 30 days, the credit bureau has not received verification from the creditor, then the credit bureau must promptly delete the credit listing.

Did you know: the burden of proof is on the consumer, not the creditor or collection agency?

Unfortunately in this credit based society one of the biggest unjust rules is that the burden of proof is on the consumer, not the creditor or collection agency.

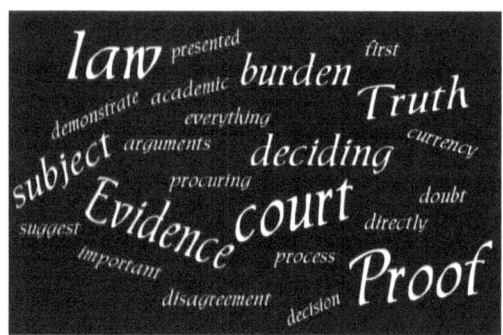

So this is how it works, the credit bureaus can basically add false information to your file at any time. They don't need any information to verify that the account is yours. Now when it is time for you to confront them and ask them why they put that on your credit report their answer is going to be "Show me the proof". They basically are holding your good credit hostage as they wait for you to provide any proof, which is at times extremely difficult. Even when a response is provided, the creditor's word is what is considered factual, not yours. So now this leaves you (the consumer) with two choices, pay off the amount to improve your credit report or ignore the item and pay higher interest rates. Sometimes it gets so bad that you are unable to obtain a line of credit. To correct credit report errors, you might have to dispute the same item multiple times and if you have the money and time and patience (which most of us working American don't) can file and manage multiple disputes at once. If you have enough money you can hire an attorney to assist you with the process. Many creditors and collection agencies will not respond until they see a letter from an attorney.

Did you know: credit bureaus want you to dispute online . . . . a huge NO,NO!?

Credit bureaus want you to dispute online because when you do that you make it easier for them and you actually waive some of your federal legal rights

1. One of those rights that you have waived is that they DO NOT have to respond to you in writing
2. Another right you have waived is that if they delete something the creditor has the right to put it back on the following month without making you aware of it
3. When you dispute an item through the mail legally they HAVE to respond within 30 days

Just when we thought they would throw us a lifeline and help a little they disguise their help as another way to hurt us. So here you are reviewing your credit report online . . . finding discrepancies . . . wanting to hurt another human being . . . and then you see it, the dispute items option. What you think is going to be the first step in fixing the problems on your report is actually the first step in the wrong direction. By submitting a dispute online it strips the consumer's legal rights, the 30-day time limit—The FCRA imposes a 30-day time limit on the dispute. If the item is not responded to within that time limit, it must be removed from your credit file. Using the automated dispute system makes it very easy for the credit-reporting bureau and reporting agency to not only respond, but to respond without having to do a full investigation . . . Under the FCRA, all relevant information must be transmitted to the data furnisher. The online dispute system circumvents that requirement.

Did you know: credit bureaus put you into different scoring categories?

The credit bureaus place you under different categories from which then they get their score, here are 2 examples . . .

- If you move a lot you are placed into a different category which lowers your score because you are viewed as unstable.
- your employment position has an effect on your credit score

  - i.e.: self employed individuals have a lower credit score than those who work for

Did you know: how your score is broken down?

- 30% of your score is debt to credit ratio
- 35% of your score is payment history
- 15% of your score is length of credit history
- 10% of your score is types of credit
- 10% of your score is the number of inquiries you have had within the last two years

Did you know: the worse the score— the more money the credit bureaus make!!?

The credit bureaus make money off your negative items being reported. Let's look at it this way; a credit card company is willing to give you a credit line. You as the consumer have poor credit, so they are going to offer this card to you with outrageous fees and inflated interest rates because you are a high-risk consumer. This credit card company WANTS people like yourself with the poor credit because they see you as willing to pay more to have a credit card because your credit is poor. People with harmed, bruised, or sub-prime credit are the people who make the banks the most amount of money in fees and interest. When verifying they are supposed to get in contact with the creditor and verify the debt. In a lot of cases they say that they have verified the account which in fact they have not. This is important to know because there are steps you can take to ensure that your account has been verified.

Did you know: why the credit bureaus want inaccurate information?

All information the creditors want to base their lending decisions off of is the most accurate information . . . . . Of course they do . . . . NOT! Creditors actually benefit when there are errors on the consumer's credit report. The worse the credit score, they more money the credit bureaus make on selling it. In addition to selling the bad data, the credit bureaus also make money on the dispute process. Let's say you went to apply for a loan. Your lender pulls your credit report and it appears you have very good credit but it is not good enough to qualify you for 0% financing. You are offered the loan at a 2.9% interest rate instead. If the approval was not automated and instead required a manual review of your credit report, you may have the opportunity to identify the items that are incorrect and provide evidence to your lender to obtain the 0% interest rate. However, the process is automated therefore actual credit reports are rarely reviewed during the process. Chances are that you will go ahead and obtain your loan at the 2.9% interest rate. The lender benefits in two ways. First, they are able to profit from the financing. Second, the calculated risk they are taking is actually lower than the credit report indicates, as you are actually a better credit risk. So why would they want accurate information, it is safe to concluded that errors that are reported on consumer's credit files benefit the lender.

Did you know: canceling credit cards can actually hurt your credit score?

Canceling credit cards can actually hurt your credit score, above all if they are an old and established part of your credit history.

Even if you no longer use a card that is extremely old, in most cases it is better to simply shred it since 15% of your score is based on the length of your history. In addition, keeping accounts open gives you a better debt to credit ratio, which makes up 30% of your credit score.

Did you know: what you can do to contest a credit item?

The Fair Credit Reporting Act (FCRA) states that you have the right to dispute incomplete or inaccurate information contained in your credit report.

The credit-reporting agency MUST investigate all inaccurate information, unless your dispute is frivolous . . . . . OF COURSE THEY FOLLOW THIS!

There is also a method outlined by the FCRA as well. Once it is identified inaccurate, incomplete, or unverifiable, information must be removed within 30 days. Finally, outdated negative information must be removed as well . . . . . Sounds great right?! Stay tuned to the next fact to see just how we the consumers still end up on the wrong side of the game that is credit scores.

Did you know: the credit bureaus use a machine to read your letters?!

New technological advances allow credit bureaus to maintain files on millions of people. Now, instead of having a person review each file the computer does it. The entire credit reporting system is now automated and lenders make credit decisions in minutes compared to what once took days or weeks.

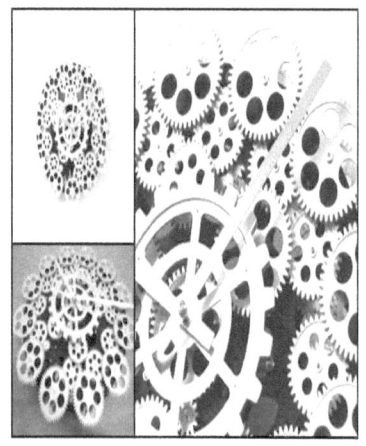

The credit bureaus use a system called E-Oscar to read the letters that you send in, A MACHINE! Your letters aren't even read by human beings.

When you send your dispute letters in it is processed by this machine which scans it and focuses on a few bits of information to sort it (name and identifying information such as social and address, codes, and text) then it gives the letter a specific code from 26 choices which include, not his/hers, account closed, account paid as agreed, etc. This is obviously faulty due to the fact that it does not present the entire issue at hand for the consumer (reminder this could be you) who is trying to fix their credit. The investigation is basically the machine determining what code your dispute falls into. Forget the fact that you have sent in supporting documentation and a detailed description of the dispute. If the machine can't read the letter then it is passed on to a human.

Did you know: there's a fourth secret credit bureau?

A fourth major credit bureau, Innovis/CBC, sometimes called the "secret credit bureau," exists! Don't be fooled that because they say "the big 3" (Equifax, Experian and TransUnion) that there are no other bureaus. Now consumers have to deal with Innovis/CBC, and dealing with them is not easy. First off Innovis/CBC is hard to find and consumers report Innovis/CBC is hesitant to provide information from its files.

Innovis/CBC is covered by FCRA and Fair and Accurate Credit Transactions Act (FACT Act). These laws require Innovis/CBC to

- provide consumers nationwide a free copy if they have been denied credit on the basis of:
    - the contents of the report
    - are unemployed and plan to seek a job
    - are on welfare
    - believe the file has inaccurate information as a result of fraud.

If you were to log onto Innovis/CBC's consumer web site you can see why they have earned the "secret credit bureau" label. The web site doesn't mention the other reasons for getting a free report under federal law. And while the "big three" credit bureaus let consumers request their free reports by phone, Internet or mail, Innovis/CBC demand that consumers write a letter and include a photocopy of their license or utility bill. Innovis/CBC does provide a toll free number, 1-800-540-2505, but the recorded message simply repeats the information found on the web site and tells consumers to request the credit report in writing.

They also don't provide information for consumers to opt-out of credit card solicitations and to opt-out of information sharing by Innovis/CBC and its affiliates. They don't tell you that you are able to opt out just like the big 3 let you; you're expected to just find this out for yourself (that's if you ever find out . . .)

Did you know: approximately 35% of your credit score is based on past debts that are over 30 days late?

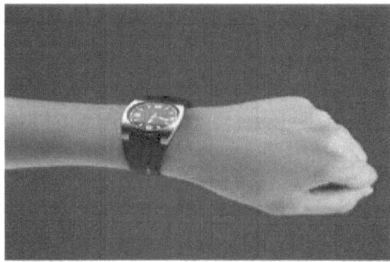

This means if for some reason you are going to be late on a payment, do not let it slip past 30 days late.

Did you know: never lie?

Never lie or falsify information about your credit score! Your credit score is easily checked by anyone and you may even face legal action for lying about it on loan applications.

Did you know: paying with cash and avoiding credit cards harms you even worse than having bad credit cards?

While not taking on any debt and paying for everything with cash seems like a logical choice for individuals who can afford this lifestyle, no credit means bad credit in the eyes of lenders. There is bound to be a time when you cannot buy something with cash, such as purchasing your first house, so make the effort to open at least one account and make purchases with the credit card occasionally.

Did you know: giving your teenager a credit card is a good choice?

Although teenagers are not always the most responsible with money, getting your child a credit card early in life can make a significant difference in the long run as it is paid off in time. There are a few excellent options for low-limit cards and prepaid cards, which will both help your child start building a positive foundation for their future credit.

Did you know: FREECREDITREPORT.COM IS NOT FREE!!!?

Avoid freecreditreport.com! It isn't free! If you want your credit report for free you can check all three major reporting companies every 12 months without any negative effects at the government sponsored site: annualcreditreport.com**

** If you use annualcreditreport.com you just waived your legal rights to receive a response from the credit bureaus from 30 days to 45 days.

3 EXTRA BONUSUS!!!
Did you know: what FDCPA violation is?

It is no secret debt collectors sometimes resort to persistent and overly aggressive tactics when attempting to collect outstanding debts. However, did you know that most of these tactics are also against the law? At both the state and federal levels, laws and statutes recognize the devious methods debt collection agents and agencies utilize to scare debtors into handing over their hard-earned money.

To curb abusive debt collection practices the federal government enacted the Fair Debt Collection Practices Act (FDCPA) in 1977. The FDCPA prohibits debt collectors from using deceitful methods to collect outstanding debts. In fact, under this law the debt collector may actually have to pay $1,000.00 dollars for violating your rights and will be forced to pay for your attorney's fees.

Debt collection agencies often use dirty tactics in an attempt to intimidate you into paying a debt you have very little means to pay. Not only is this unfair, but also unreasonable. Seldom do debt collectors take into account your current standard of living and the people that depend on you for the basic necessities of life. When a debt collector is being deceitful when speaking with you or communicates threats and harasses you, they have broken the law and should be held accountable.

If a debt collection agent or agency has ever threatened you in any way, you may be entitled to file a lawsuit against the debt collection company or law firm to protect your consumer rights and pursue compensation for damages.

Some examples of illegal debt collection tactics:

- Calling too early in the morning before 8 A.M. or too late at night after 9 P.M.
- Telephone calls to your mobile phone made from an auto-dialer.
- Using profane language when attempting to collect.
- Threatening you in any manner.
- Not revealing their identity.
- Suing on a time-barred debt.
- Misrepresenting the debt in any way.
- Contacting you when you are represented by an attorney.
- Contacting third parties regarding your debt.

Did you know: who or what are junk buyers?

The vast majority of the lawsuits filed in the County Court system are for what is known as "junk debt." Junk Debt is a multi-billion dollar industry involving charged-off debt which is often sold to large investors or similar enterprises for pennies on the dollar in the hope of turning a lucrative profit. The junk debt buyer is permitted to collect upon or sue for the entire value of the debt, not just what they paid for it. These "junk debt buyers" purchase large portfolios of delinquent or charged-off accounts from credit card companies, or even other collection agencies.

These companies fall under the Fair Debt Collection Practices Act, 15 U.S.C. § 1692, definition of a "collection agency" and are subject to all penalties therein. As the visibility and profitability of this rapidly expanding new industry has grown, junk debt buyers range in size from small private businesses up to multi-million dollar, publicly traded Wall Street companies. Credit card debt accounts for nearly 70% percent of the accounts sold to junk debt buyers, followed by auto loans, telecommunications debt and retail accounts. If the junk debt buyer is unsuccessful in collection upon the debt after systematically harassing you with letters and telephone calls, they will often resort to the filing of a lawsuit against you.

Junk debt buyers generally buy alleged debts for cents on the dollar and then attempt to find ways to collect on the debt. Often times, the debt is "time-barred" (That is, the statute of limitations on it has expired and it no longer legally needs to be repaid). The buyer then attempts to get the debtor to pay a small portion of the debt. If the debtor does so, they have reaffirmed the debt and started the statute of limitations over again. It is very important that consumers be aware of their rights and the laws that protect them as an alarmingly large number of these debt buyers are barely operating within the law. Many consumers often ask.

Did you know: what is the statue of limitations on debt?

Unfortunately, there is no hard and fast rule. While some lawyers often state the general rule that the Statue of Limitations in Florida is 4 or 5 years depending upon the nature of the debt and if there is a signed contract.

Frequently in these situations, the junk debt buyer will use the practice of "re-aging" an account which basically means that they report it as more recent than it really is. In addition to a Statute of Limitations defense, many consumers will also have additional legal defenses, such as the failure of the debt buyer to comply with what is known in the law as a "condition precedent". This means that if the person suing you failed to follow a certain procedure or perform a particular act, a competent lawyer can have your entire lawsuit dismissed.

Finally, many debt collectors, especially the junk debt buyers, may have difficulty proving details regarding a debt. In Florida, every Plaintiff in a civil case has to prove their case by a preponderance of the evidence, often referred to as the "burden of proof." Junk Debt Buyers are often unable to meet this burden due to a lack of paperwork, the fact that the debt was previously paid off, or an unrelated act, such as identity theft.

Most importantly, never ignore the lawsuit even if you do not recognize the party suing you! If you do not defend the lawsuit, you lose—plain and simple. Always consult an attorney to apprise you of your legal rights.

CHECK OUT MY NEXT BOOK WHICH WILL BE A DID YOU KNOW ABOUT 3RD PARTY COLLECTION COMPANIES (AKA junk debt buyers) WHICH SUES THOUSANDS OF INDIVIDUALS EVERY MONTH AND HOW YOU CAN FIGHT BACK!! KNOW YOUR LEGAL RIGHT!!

The Next Step

NEED MORE HELP GETTING YOUR CREDIT FIXED???

Contact the Author of this book for more information, consultation is completely free! Take the next steps towards a debt free life.

Mark Guerrero
Credit Repair Solutions
1-888-264-5113
crsonline@hotmail.com
www.creditrepairsolutionsonline.com

www.ingramcontent.com/pod-product-compliance
Lightning Source LLC
Chambersburg PA
CBHW021928170526
45157CB00005B/2229